Your Background is Not the Ultimate: God Knows Your Future

Before I formed you in the womb I knew you; before you were born I sanctified you; I ordained you a prophet to the nations. (Jeremiah 1:5)

Ferdinand Senyo Lawson

2012

Published by
Ferdinard Senyo Lawson
No. 24 Onyasia Crescent
Roman Ridge
Accra, Ghana
Email: ferdinardl@hotmail.com
Tel: 00 233 0243493859/0244987452
   0044-7958500337/ 0044-7538034723 (UK)

© Copyright Ferdinard Senyo Lawson 2012

All rights reserved. No part of this book may be reproduced or transmitted in any form or by any means, electronic or mechanical, including photocopying, recording, or by any information storage and retrieval system, without the prior permission in writing from the publishers.

To
All the men and women who in the past
were written off but who through the word of
God, now have a successful and impactful life.

My late grandmother, Felicia Ami Ocloo,
who never gave up on me but believed in my future,
Grandma may your soul rest in perfect peace

My parents

My beloved wife, Mrs. Deborah Zara Lawson

and

My precious children, Prince Joshua Seyram-Yao
and Princess Jessica Senam-Yawah Lawson,
who have inspired me to complete this book.

God bless you all.

Contents

Acknowledgement v

Preface vii

Introduction ix

1. Take a Step of Faith 1

2. Renew Your Mind: Don't Dwell on the Past 10

3. God Will Turn Your Situation Around 23

4. Chase Your Dream 30

5. No More Limitations 42

6. Don't Give Up: You Have A Sure Future 61

7. Be Still: God Is Fighting For You 70

References 85

Acknowledgement

I give all the glory to the Lord God almighty for revealing himself to me and giving me his word to share with this generation and the generation unborn. It is an opportunity to contribute to what other men of God have written through experience, to encourage the body of Christ.

My sincere thanks go to my destiny father, Bishop Michael Hutton-Wood, the Senior Pastor of the House of Judah (Praise) Ministries, who himself is a writer. He has the mandate to raise generational leaders to impact nations, by empowering men and women to release their full potential to maximize their destiny. Bishop, may God bless you for believing in us that we can all fulfill our destiny. You never gave up on anybody but kept preaching the word of God to us. Thank you for your input in my personal life.

I express my profound gratitude to my spiritual mentor, Pastor Charles Owusu of the Deeper Christian Life Bible Church, Ghana, for being an inspirational and life coach to me. God bless you.

Finally, I thank all brothers and sisters in the body of Christ, especially the members of House of Judah Praise Ministry for their unfailing prayers. May God increase you all.

Preface

By the grace of God and his divine direction, I have managed to put material together so that anybody who reads this book will be encouraged and motivated to look to the future rather than being limited by their unfavourable backgrounds.

This book will also serve as a driving force to encourage all believers that whatever negative experiences they have had, no condition is permanent but they will be all that God has called them to be only if they would allow the word of God to transform and reshape their mindset, then will they realize that negative backgrounds do not matter.

This book is intended to help people to overcome their hurtful past and develop self-confidence in pursuing their purpose.

Regardless of your past history, your future is a fresh page to start afresh. God knows your future.

Introduction

"The glory of this latter house shall be greater than the former, saith the LORD of hosts: and in this place will I give peace, saith the LORD of hosts" (Haggai 2:9)

Sometimes, events that happen in our life make us feel tired, burdened, or regretful. Interestingly, most of us spend too much time thinking about horrible and dreadful situations we may have been involved in or deeds we have committed, even though there is no chance that we can change them.

Our individual lives are purely determined by our past, present or future. Many people's lives are driven by their past regrets, disappointments, failures and betrayals which hold them back from seeing the bright future ahead of them.

It is therefore crucial that we develop the attitude and mindset to learn from those bad experiences so as to rise above any form of negative background issues that try to hold us or limit our progress in life. God's purpose for your life is not limited by your past. It is through our past failures that we develop and learn much about how to succeed and how not to fail again; something George Orwell agrees with, when he says, "He who controls the past also controls the future."

Background can be termed as one's family origin, level of education, experiences etc. that contribute to an individual's present character and status. It can also be referred to as a person's history, places lived, jobs held or memories. Our background is very unique because it determines who we are and why we are the way we are: positive or negative.

Your background or your state does not really matter — is it a physical handicap, (blindness, deafness, or crippled limbs) or educational levels, poor performance at school?

You can be all that the Lord God has made you to be only if you can put your trust daily in God, knowing that he is the God of second chances. He will use your negatives past hurts to transform you, for ". . . we know that all things work together for good to them that love God, to them who are the called according to his purpose." (Romans 8:28) today to create your desired future."

Therefore, it is purely up to us what we do about the present which will surely determine our forward movement. Apostle Paul had to forget about the past and try to embrace the future.

"One thing I do, forgetting those things which are behind and reaching forward to those things which are ahead, I press toward the goal for the prize of the upward call of God in Jesus name."

As mentioned earlier, every one of us is bound to experiences of unhappiness in our lives, unpleasant memories and perhaps some really painful ones. Whatever it is, you need to forget the negative past and move on. "Forget the former things; do not dwell on the past. See the Lord is saying he is doing a new thing! Now it springs up; do you not perceive it? He is making a way in the desert and streams in the wasteland," says Isaiah 43:18-19.

"The future is what you make it and not what you think it should be but is created by those who turn their adversity into advantage and do not allow their past to hold their life hostage, so says Bishop Hutton-Wood.

As I researched this write-up, I came across

some people who actually confirmed that their negative backgrounds especially their upbringing still controls their present life, and they find it difficult to let go. Clearly, their upbringing has had a negative impact on them.

Our backgrounds determine the way we all live our lives. For some, their parents tried their best to raise them. However, some parents lacked the patience, time and effort needed to be proper parents. People with disciplined backgrounds tend to be disciplined too. Some also grew up in abusive and neglected homes.

Nevertheless, with God all things are possible only if the individuals are ready and prepared to move forward from those negative experiences and hurts. It is only then that they can create the very future they want, for as says Bishop Hutton-Wood says, "The future is created by those who make every experience, be it positive or negative, work to their full benefit."

The story of Jabez is a clear indication that negative background or history affects an individual's life; but taking control of those situations allows you to progress in life.

The Bible indicates that Jabez was born into

negative circumstances, (hardship, pains and sorrowful upbringing). His own mother called him "sorrowful one," meaning sorrowful events because she said, "I bare him in sorrow, and pain."

The story in 1 Chronicles 4:9-10, states that from the birth of Jabez, things were not very good at all for his mother and siblings. They were all placed in some messed-up, terrible circumstances. Therefore his mother naming him Jabez, meant she was actually confirming the hard future of her son.

Praise God, her prediction about his son did not manifest. Do you know why? Because as Jabez grew up, he recognised and acknowledged that God is the only pillar that holds up his life and future and that no man can decide, design, discover or even predict his future. He also had a revelation about himself that even if nobody believed in him, he believed in himself. He encouraged himself and that motivated him out of the negative circumstances he was born into. He kept believing in himself and took the steps of faith against whatever prediction and stigma were attached to his destiny.

Yes, your background may not have been a

good one, but as you discover yourself in the Lord and believe the word of God above the words of men, you can take control and drive your destiny according to the purpose God has destined for you.

Maybe you have been labelled a failure or are not supposed to be anything good. It does not matter the meaning of your name; it could also mean that your future is supposed to be full of sorrow, but you can say like Jabez "I refuse to live in sorrow! "I reject all manner of sorrow!"

The circumstances in which you grew up may not permit you to make it, but say to yourself "I'm going to make it in life. I'm going to be great and be all that God has created me to be."

Do not allow your negative backgrounds to stop or limit your progress in life or hinder you from pursuing your purpose, because, "The future is secured by those whose lives are driven by their very purpose."

Be driven by your purpose and do not allow the colour of your skin, for example, limit your capacity to achieve great things. The word of God encourages us that we can do all things through Christ Jesus who strengthens us. Therefore point to your negative events and command them to leave you alone, because you are destined for greatness.

In the journey to greatness, there will be various attacks from people you know or who knew your childhood days and will try to remind you of those painful and sorrowful events. They may even call you by some names as they see you approaching but as someone has said, "Yesterday is history, tomorrow, a mystery. today is a gift."

"Don't get bitter but get better" advises Bishop Michael Hutton-Wood. All you need to do is to identify your background and pray to God for a change of story. As you do so, God will hear your prayer and change your situation and will definitely empower you with the ability to shine.

Whatever the circumstances that are attached to your name, your birth or your place of birth, they cannot dictate the course of your life. Rising above the negative past will always gain you a better reputation for being "more honourable than your friends and brethren."

Truly, your background does not matter. I promise you if, yesterday you were disappointed, today you are approved, tomorrow you will be appointed.

1

Take a Step of Faith

Faith is taking the first step, even when you don't see the whole staircase. (Martin Luther King Jr.)

Faith, as has been aptly described by the quotation above involves the act of trusting. Taking the step of faith simply means believing that whatever the word of God has said concerning you is true and without physically seeing the evidence, you see that thing with spiritual eyes that it will come to pass in your life. Faith is hoping, trusting and believing in the goodness and trustworthiness of God.

Faith is being obedient to what you believe you were called to do and being "sure of what we hope for and certain of what we do not see," (Heb. 11:1).

But to believe in something and not do anything to see it manifest in your life is not acting in faith. After you have believed in something positive about your future, it is your full responsibility to act, work, and deploy your senses to obtain what you want.

Discovering your purpose, dreams and vision alone is not enough; you actually need to take positive steps to see those dreams come true. As French novelist, Anatole France says, "To accomplish great things, we must dream as well as act."

You may have had a negative background or horrible circumstances when you were growing up. Those events may be very hurtful in your memory — you need to take steps, make a conscious decision and employ measures, to avoid those events happening again in your life.

You have the power to change things to favour you. But for that to happen, you need to develop your confidence and belief in the word of God concerning you, because "Without faith, it is impossible to please God," (Hebrews 11:6).

Having the knowledge about the importance of water to your body and believing that water is very good to your kidney as well but not taking the step to go and get the water to drink is not acting on the knowledge and that is not faith either.

Faith without works is dead. Whatever and wherever you are now is subject to change— that is if you are not happy with the situation. No condition is permanent. It takes the step of faith to pray to God to see result.

You may have had a terrible upbringing but once you discover that you are not very happy about your life you should act on God's word and do positive things to turn things to your favour.

God's promise is that, " . . . all things work together for good to them that love God, to them who are the called according to his purpose," (Romans 8:28). God has a purpose for your life and the gates of hell cannot stop you from achieving that goal, and no matter your family background or any prediction given by people, you will be successful in Jesus' name.

Abraham is referred to as the father of faith for "By faith Abraham, when called to go to a place he would later receive as his inheritance, obeyed and went, even though he did not know where he was going. By faith he made his home in the Promised Land like a stranger in a foreign country; he lived in tents, as did Isaac and Jacob, who were heirs with him of the same promise. For he was looking forward to the city with foundations, whose architect and builder is God," (Heb. 11:8-10).

Abraham believed in God's word to him and to follow his footsteps and take the steps of faith, there is the need to read the word of God concerning you. Faith comes by hearing, and hearing by the word of God. God's word which you hear will activate joy inside you to hold onto God's sure promises for your destiny. This is to say that faith in God's word produces inner joy, as Jesus promised in John 15:11 that, "These things have I spoken unto you, that my joy might remain in you, and that your joy might be full."

So no matter what you are going through in life as a result of your negative history or backgrounds, the word of God encourages you to count it all joy because joy is the driving force to victory in Jesus' name. Adversity will come but it is only those who have maintained their joy who will enjoy the victory.

Your circumstances may not be palatable but remember that God has not left you or forsaken you. It is your attitude and the steps of faith you take in God's word against those negative issues that will empower you to overcome and have a fruitful future.

Life itself is full of struggles and one can say that without struggle, a person cannot develop his or her full potential. Have you ever watched an ant carrying home a piece of bread that is bigger than it? This means that regardless of the size of an ant, nothing is too big for it to carry as far as its faith is concerned. So faith enables a person to surmount problems no matter how big they are.

If God the Creator lives within you, then *you* who have been created in his image, are also creative. That means when you cannot find a job, you should take a step of faith to go out there and create your own job. This is to say that, if success does not come to you, get you up and go find it! As someone has said, "Success belongs to those who are too small to carry what they believe in; but too big to leave it behind."

Once you discover your purpose, dreams and gifts, take the step of faith and develop that dream or gift into fulfillment. Do not wait for opportunity because the opportunity is the breath in your body and the strength in mind.

In Deuteronomy 8:18, we discover that God does not give us wealth; but he empowers us to get wealth. Taking the step of faith forbids you from sitting down and waiting for honey to drop onto your tongue for you to lick.

As Bishop David Oyedepo once said, "Success does not fall on people's lap but [comes] through the act of faith and self-development."

This means that a dream without a definite corresponding action only irritates and aggravates your soul and amounts to nothing.

Maybe you did something really wrong, and your current situation is the result of that mistake. Take responsibility for your mistakes but blaming yourself will only put weight on that past and drag you down. It's all in the past. You are in the present now and you can do something about it.

LET US RECAP:

❶ Remember, it does not matter what happened to you in the past; if you can begin to renew your mind and take the step of faith to create the future you really want then God will give you the power to succeed.

❷ Take the step of faith in believing God's word concerning you rather than what men have "prophesied" over your life.

❸ Don't allow your background to hinder, prevent, or limit you from achieving your full potential.

❹ Refuse to accept any form of rejection from family and friends and see God as the only one who can secure your destiny.

❺ Nevertheless, faith doesn't only mean believing God will provide or God will show you the way. It means taking an actual "step of faith" in the direction you believe God is leading you.

My brother, my sister in the Lord, the following verses and quotations of encouragement should put a great smile on your face.

> There is surely a future hope for you, and your hope will not be cut off. (PROVERBS 23:18 NIV)

> Be of good courage, and he shall strengthen your heart, all ye that hope in the LORD. (PSALM 31:24 KJV)

> My brethren, count it all joy when ye fall into divers temptation; knowing this, that the trying of your faith worketh patience. (JAMES 1:2-3)

> Understanding of God's word is all that faith requires to come alive and you do not need more than God to have all your needs met. (BISHOP OYEDEPO)

> God is all you need to have all your needs met; and faith is all it takes to get God to work.

> Don't laugh at me, my enemies. Although I've fallen, I will get up. Although I sit in the dark, the LORD is my light (MICAH 7:8)

> Go your way, eat the fat, and drink the sweet, and send portions unto them for whom nothing is prepared: for this day is holy unto our Lord: neither be ye sorry; for the joy of the LORD is your strength. (NEHEMIAH 8: 9-10)

You are born to win. You cannot be defeated when you take a step of faith to develop yourself in God's word and take practical steps to develop yourself to your desired end. The devil is a losing liar.

YOU ARE THE WINNER.

2

Renew Your Mind: Don't Dwell on the Past

And do not be conformed to this world, but be transformed by the renewing of your mind, that you may prove what is that good and acceptable and perfect will of God. (ROMANS 12:2)

It is very necessary to note that until an individual renews and changes his or her mind about their unfavourable background experiences, their dreams are not going to materialise because our minds can be influenced by negative thoughts from our background.

Everything we do is by choice and if you want to see a change in your personal life, it is necessary that you change the way you view things. Until you are willing to renew your mind daily, minute by minute i.e. practise changing the way your mind looks at everything with the word of God concerning your destiny, you will see little and your future will be controlled by negative experiences.

"The secret of your future is hidden in your daily routine therefore be careful about what occupies your mind because it will greatly determine what you will become tomorrow," so says Bishop Michael Hutton-Wood.

The terrible truth is that many of us, even though we are born again and Holy Ghost-filled, still live in misery, carrying over the past and letting that pull us back.

An unrenewed mindset leads to depression that can sometimes lead to suicidal thoughts. This is to say that being born again alone doesn't mean that you are going to prevent negative memories coming into your mind or having depressing feelings. They are all still going to be there. That is why you need to renew your mind daily with the sure word of God.

Romans 12:1-2 teaches us what we must do: "I beseech you therefore, brethren, by the mercies of God, that you present your bodies a living sacrifice, holy and acceptable to God. And do not be conformed to this world, but be transformed by the renewing of your mind, that you may prove to be what is good and acceptable and perfect in the will of God."

When you got born again God gave you a brand new godly heart, as Ezekiel 36:26-27 tells us, "Moreover, I will give you a new heart and put a new Spirit within you; and I will remove the heart of stone from your flesh and give you a heart of flesh. And I will put my Spirit within you."

However, it is when you combine that new heart with a brand new mindset that you will have awesome and incredible Godly changes taking place in your life and you will be on your way to good success.

Remember that your mind has control over every single action you make—your mind controls your thoughts; your mind tells your body exactly what to do; it tells your mouth what words to speak; it tells your eyes what to look at; it tells your ears what things to pay attention to and what things to tune out; it tells your brain what to think about; it tells your entire being how to respond in every single situation. That is why it is vital that you renew your mindset each day with God's word against bad memory, depressive feelings, and everything that takes your focus off God and places it on you and your problems.

Furthermore, your mind is the foundation of your intellect which really controls your personal self-esteem and drives you to succeed. It is true that sometimes we are faced with some thoughts that we have no control over, but you can actually determine what dwells in you and controls your lifestyle.

Bishop Michael Hutton-Wood,* tells us that the best way to deal with and forget about your negative experiences is to become fruitful and occupy yourself with productive thinking to produce something positive to impact nations.

It does not matter your background of failures and shortcomings, when you begin to renew your mindset by changing the way you see yourself, you can embark on the road to achievement.

Everyone has a past; but we should never allow our negative past to get in the way of our

---

* Check out his book, *How to Negotiate Your Desired Future with Today's Currency*

future. But God's promises are always assuring. He promises to be with us and never to forsake us, but to give us victory and rest (Exodus 33:14). Therefore there is no reason why you should feel intimidated by your negative conditions and not to be bold enough to face life like Peter who dared to walk on the water.

George Orwell, said, "He who controls the past controls the future." In other words, he who ignores the past is condemned to repeat it. So it is necessary that you discipline what goes through your mind so as to move on. Learn from the past by all means, but be like Apostle Paul, "One thing I do, forgetting those things which are behind, and reaching forth unto those things which are before," (Philippians 3:13).

The Psalmist says, "I will praise the Lord, for I am fearfully and wonderfully made." Encourage yourself that your birth is not an accident, you are not just born to add to the earth's population. The word of God says that you are a royal priesthood and a peculiar person, you are born to fill a gap and therefore you *are* unique. You have the mind of Christ and all it takes to be great. Just discover who you are in Christ and then you can recover your true self to accomplish greater things, "For as a man thinketh in his heart, so is he," (Proverbs 23:7)

Dr. Walter Staples says, "The key to success lies in your particular manner of thinking. When you change how you think about yourself, your relationships, your goals, and your world, your life changes. If you change the quality of your thinking, you necessarily will change the quality of your life."

Therefore be very careful about what you allow to control your mind and what you think about. What you think about surely becomes your character and identity. No matter how poor your background was, whether you were neglected or are down trodden, you have what it takes to be at the top.

Your happiness depends primarily on your attitude in life, and especially on the nature and quality of your thoughts and ideas, which are more powerful than you may imagine. They are your main weapons in your fight for a better life. You only see the world as your mind sees it. In other words, all your perceptions and thoughts act as a filter between reality and you. The world is what you think it is. If you think it is bad, you won't be able to make progress. You'll be happy or unhappy depending on whether your thoughts are positive or negative. To make your ideas as powerful as possible, they have to be positive. When a negative idea enters your mind, use the sure word of God to get rid of it.

Your thoughts influence your existence, as well as your environment. Your chosen dream (vision, purpose, and goal) demands the right environment or climate to materialise. It is very vital that you control your environment or the atmosphere around your dream or that atmosphere will definitely control you. This is to say that the individual climate we create knowingly or unknowingly determines and influences our behaviour and decisions.

It does not matter the environment in which you grew up; as long as you are prepared and ready to change that negative atmosphere with the word of God, you can be assured that you will make progress. How you see controls your mind and your desire. If you see yourself as great and powerful then you will do the right things to bring those dreams to pass in your life.

Therefore do not sit down and wait or hope that somebody else is going to make things happen for you. You have to take control of what goes into your mind. Begin to invest into your future and the environment that inspires you toward excellence and the improvement of your life.

We should make sure our minds think the way the word of God says in Romans 12:2, "*Be* not conformed to this world but *be* transformed by the renewing of your mind." The "be" is a commandment rather than a suggestion. We do not have a choice, we need to work on it.

The word "conform" means to assume an outward expression that does not come from an inward being. In other words, when you conform to something you feel so much influence that you begin to change the way you act. When you begin to conform to this world system, you are not being faithful to who you really are on the inside. Behind the world system, there is the evil one.

"Transform" means to assume an outward expression that comes from the inward being. This transformation needs to take place in our minds. The Bible cautions us that the carnal mind in itself is enmity against God. The transformation comes from the word of God.

When you read the word of God from the pages of the Bible and ponder over it, it gets into your mind and goes down into your spirit. When you keep doing this, you can see your mind lining up with your spirit. That is the key. Otherwise, a constant battle that goes on between your mind and your spirit.

We all are eternal beings with eternal spirits, we live in a mortal body and we have a soul that is made up of the mind, will and emotions. The only doorway for the enemy into your soul is through your mind. Everything starts with a thought. Before you attempt to do anything, you think about it first. Your mind is the doorway to your deeds. Proverbs 23:7 says, "As a man thinks in his heart, so is he."

You cannot have a happy life if you have a sad mind; you need a healthy mind. Our mind is what makes us the person God made us to be.

It is so important to guard our thought life because Isaiah 26:3 says, "If you will keep your mind stayed on Me, I will hold you in perfect peace." Situations and circumstances change all the time. If our minds focus on the things that are changing day by day, our life will be like a boat in a storm. That is why it is so important we have an anchor. You will never wage a successful battle unless you have a personal relationship with the Lord Jesus Christ.

It is my fervent prayer that as you begin to renew your mind about your life you will be like the stars which do not struggle to shine and like a river which does not struggle to flow. You will not struggle to excel in life and fulfill your purpose on earth in Jesus name.

LET US RECAP:

❶ Remember also that no matter how hard you try, you cannot change the past, but definitely you can make a better future for yourself.

❷ Your life today is as result of what you thought of yesterday. It is very important that we really watch what goes through our minds especially the negative experiences that keep coming into our mind, and take control of it by renewing it daily.

❸ Renewing your mind with the word of God concerning your destiny gives you assurance which then promotes your confidence in your ability to pursue great things in life.

❹ Renewal of mind is a continuous process. Paul says in Ephesians 4:23 that we should "Be renewed in the spirit of [...]our mind'. We need to work our way through with our minds. The new man always contrasts the old life style therefore we must make every effort to renew our minds.

❺ Your atmosphere will often determine your productivity in life. Our thoughts influence our existence, as well as our environment. You'll be happy or unhappy depending on whether your thoughts are positive or negative.

❻ Remember that in life, relationships do not last forever; therefore it is very important that when people leave your life, you should never get angry, bitter or regretful. Just motivate yourself to do better than when they left you. Whatever the case you are more precious to your generation than what people think you are.

Some Quotations to Encourage You:

> Never underestimate the power of dreams and the influence of the human spirit. (WILMA RUDOLPH)

> Give me now wisdom and knowledge that I may go out and come in before this people: for who can judge this thy people that is so great? (2 CHRONICLES 1:10)

> Never give up, for that is just the place and time that the tide will turn. (HARRIET BEECHER STOWE)

> The future is created by those who don't have everyone as a friend. (BISHOP MICHAEL HUTTON-WOOD)

> Nobody else can create your atmosphere for you. (MIKE MURDOCK)

> Fear not; for thou shalt not be ashamed: neither be thou confounded; for thou shalt not be put to shame: for thou shalt forget the shame of thy youth, and shalt not remember the reproach of thy widowhood any more. (ISAIAH 54:4)

> We do not wrestle against flesh and blood, but against principalities, against powers, against the evil rulers of this dark world. (EPHESIANS 6:12)

> When we sow in our weakness on our knees, we reap in strength on our feet. (UNKNOWN)

A meaningless life is worse than cancer. If you desire a meaningful and a successful life, you must begin to renew your mind and embrace your future.

YOUR LIFE IS WHAT YOU MAKE IT 👍

3

God Will Turn Your Situation Around

Behold I will do a new thing, Now it shall spring forth; shall you not know it? I will even make a road in the wilderness and rivers in the desert. (Isaiah 43:19)

God is in the business of changing and turning people's life around by giving them not only a second chance, but a fresh start.

It is possible to say that in life, pain and problems come to everyone at one stage in their lives. As believers, we are encouraged that God is our helper and that he will see us through life's challenges. God has promised that He will never leave us nor forsake us (Deuteronomy 31: 5) and that he will fight our battles (2 Chronicles 20:15). That is not to say that trouble will not come to us all but God will be there to help us through those difficult times.

According to Bishop Hutton-Wood, whatever the attacks from the enemy God will turn it around for your good. God turns tests into testimony, and adversity into victorious adventure, as well as mess into message. God also turns people's failures into triumphs and their disappointments into divine appointments.*

Praise God, for he says, ". . . I know the thoughts that I think toward you, saith the LORD, thoughts of peace, and not of evil, to give you an expected end. (Jeremiah 29:11 KJV)

God's word encourages us that even if we walk through the valley of the shadow of death, the Lord God will be with us. He, the Lord will turn our negative backgrounds around to our favour.

The Bible teaches, "For his anger endureth but a moment; in his favour is life: weeping may endure for a night, but joy cometh in the morning." (Psalm 30:5)

---

* Get the full illustration from the Bishop's book, *How to Negotiate Your Desired Future With Today's Currency*.

Hannah, the wife of Elkanah, was barren and was mocked by Peninnah, her rival. It came to pass that as Hannah went up to worship in Shiloh, she cried before the Lord and made a vow to the Lord God almighty that if he would give her a son, she would give him back to God. God granted her wish and turned Hannah's weeping into joy.

He is still in the business of turning our weeping into joy. He did the same for Joseph. One night Joseph was in prison, the next day he was in the palace.

God has not changed. What he did for Hannah and Joseph, he can do for you, for as Luke 1:37, says ". . . nothing is impossible for God." He can heal our bodies, our minds and even change the events of our life, for nothing is impossible for Him.

There are so many places in the Bible where God actually changed the past. Consider all those whom he raised from the dead, the most famous and well-known being Jesus Christ himself, in the glorious resurrection.

We all make mistakes, but at times it can feel like we are trapped. The solutions for our problems can sometimes seem worse than the problems themselves.

Perhaps you have done the wrong thing and made some wrong choices regarding your life or maybe you have done what you knew you should not do and now you are suffering the consequences of those mistakes. Let me assure you that regardless of any mistake you have made in the past or the tragedy that has come into your life, if you will turn to God, he is prepared to take your mistakes, your awful circumstance, and turn it into a miracle.

Now the question is, do you keep reliving your past mistakes and failures? Many in the body of Christ are trapped in their 'yesterday' events. It is so sad that many of us also never move on in our walk with the Lord, forgetting that God offers freedom and deliverance regardless of our bondage or negative circumstance. It is time to rely on God to turn things in your favour.

The almighty God wants us to have assurance that no matter how much evil and suffering and futility we see now, he will make all things new.

Joseph's brothers sold him out of hatred and he was taken to a foreign country. People lied about him, and as a result, he was thrown into prison. Many bad things happened to Joseph. But God took care of him through it all and in the end he became the prime minister of Egypt.

That God has not changed. He can do the same thing for you. Regardless of the circumstance you are in, with God on your side, you cannot lose. And we know that all things work together for good to them that love God, to them who are the called according to his purpose. (Romans 8:28)

"All things" include your failures, your mistakes, your background and even the attacks of the devil. If you will pray and seek God's face for a turn-around you will see the hand of God moving in your direction. No matter what life may have thrown your way, you can be more than a conqueror through him who loves you.

LET US RECAP:

❶ Bad choices always lead to bad decisions; the choices you make in life either make you or break you.

❷ Though your mistakes can lead to circumstances and troubles that seem very grim, God can turn your mistakes into miracles.

❸ The Lord took all the tragedies in Joseph's life

and turned them into a fantastic miracle that not only blessed Joseph but ended up saving the lives of his family and countless others in the land of Egypt and throughout the known world.

Some Quotations to Encourage You:

> If my people, which are called by my name, shall humble themselves, and pray, and seek my face, and turn from their wicked ways; then will I hear from heaven, and will forgive their sin, and will heal their land. (2 CHRONICLE 7:14)

> Wherefore seeing we also are compassed about with so great a cloud of witnesses, let us lay aside every weight, and the sin which doth so easily beset us, and let us run with patience the race that is set before us." (KJV)

When a man lifts you up, it's definitely to the height of his hands, but when God lifts you up it is limitless. Seek him now and forsake all else and your situation will never be the same.

YOU WILL BE UPLIFTED FOREVER!!! 👍

4

Chase Your Dream

> *And David inquired at the LORD, saying, Shall I pursue after this troop? Shall I overtake them? And he answered him, Pursue: for thou shalt surely overtake them, and without fail recover all.* (1 SAMUEL 30:8 NKJV)

God always wants a family relationship with you since he is your father. God has a purpose and a plan for your life. In Hebrews 10:7, we learn that we are created for a specific purpose and as we identify that purpose and plan for our lives, we can then live to fulfill the agenda of God for our lives and be all that God has created us to be — to impact nations and maximise destiny.

You need to have a plan by actually sitting

down and counting the cost involved in achieving the dream. Having a dream, plan,or vision alone is not enough. You need to count the cost — which is another thing all together. Jesus asked, "For who of you, willing to build a tower, doth not first, having sat down, count the expenses, whether he has the things for completing?"(Luke 14:28)

To be able to live a life full of impact, it is very important that you discover your purpose for living and do every positive thing to see it come true.

To start with, what does it mean to have a vision for life? Some define vision as having a purpose, goal or dream, while others differentiate between vision and purpose.

Let us now look at vision (as purpose) to drive home what we really want to understand. Having a vision or purpose for your life actually means being determined or persuaded to do or achieve something positive in life through definitive decision making. Daniel did so: "But Daniel purposed in his heart that he would not defile himself with the portion of the king's meat, nor with the wine which he drank: therefore he requested the prince of the eunuchs that he might not defile himself," (Daniel 1:8)

Have a dream or goal set before you and keep your eyes on that goal and be not easily distracted by any sounds or individuals along the way to fulfilling that purpose. Make up your mind to stand firm whether somebody encourages you or not; make a conscious decision to see that dream come to pass in your life.

A purposeful person is the one who is able to buy the truth and sell it not —who has made up his mind to hold onto the truth and withstand evil. Such a person is not moved by detractors but keeps sailing to the directions he has to overcome. To be able to succeed in life and impact nations, you need to deny yourself certain things that do not correspond with your purpose. You actually deny yourself from pleasures because you know your purpose for your life and focus on your dream.

Daniel's purpose was not to defile himself with the king's meat. He knew that the consequences of not eating the king's meat are so great but he denied himself in order to please God.

He was in Babylon, away from home, but he had principles and determination to please God —that was his sole purpose. His parents were not there to assure him neither were there any other family members to persuade him to comply with the customs of Babylon.

It is very important that we stand firm for the dream or vision we have. There may be dangers around you to persuade you to go against your purpose but hold on to that purpose and the dream, in the process of time, as you work smartly, you will achieve your aim.

The advice in 2 Corinthians 4:18 encourages us — "While we look not at the things which are seen, but at the things which are not seen: for the things which are seen are temporal; but the things which are not seen are eternal." If you are not moved by the challenges and discouragements from loved ones or the devil's tricks to abort your dream you will realise that those challenges were nothing compared to your fulfillment in life.

You make your mind to hold unto God's promises through his word that nothing can separate you from your purpose and you will achieve the purpose for which that dream was given to you. You need to encourage yourself in the Lord as David did.

There is the need to watch and pray

concerning your purpose and dreams and ensure these drive your spirit man daily, because there is a tendency to lose focus on that dream. You need to protect and guide your purpose because not many people out there are happy about your dreams of getting university education, attaining business success, getting your dream home or marrying your beloved partner. There are some pharaohs in our present day who are looking to destroy that baby — your dream.

The story of Joseph in Genesis is a classic example of dreams and the challenges that can hinder their fulfillment. Joseph's brothers were already jealous of his privileged positon in the family and so when he told them his dreams which suggested he would be placed above them, they plotted and sold him into slavery into Egypt. His gift of interpretation of dreams brought him to Pharaoh's attention. He saved Egypt and the surrounding countries (and his brothers and father) from famine.

The conclusion of this story is that you should beware where and how you share dreams. However, if you have shared your dreams with your loved ones and you are suffering as a result of it, there is hope for you. No matter the consequences resulting from sharing those dreams, God is your protector; he will protect you and your dreams will be realised.

"Trust in the LORD with all thine heart; and lean not unto thine own understanding. In all thy ways acknowledge him, and he shall direct thy paths," so says Proverbs 3:5-6.

In pursuit of your purpose, dream or vision, it is very important that you identify your personal strengths and weaknesses. By so doing, you identify the steps you need to take and improve upon, to actually see that purpose being fulfilled.

You cannot say that you have a dream and do not know what, when and how that dream can be achieved. You need to have the knowledge about what to do regarding that vision. Many of us are destroyed even though we have dreams and ambition because we lack knowledge which is the power for success, just as Hosea 4:6 says, "My people are destroyed for lack of knowledge. . ."

King Solomon needed knowledge in pursuing his vision, goal and purpose as a king. He knew that without knowledge and a discerning heart to govern God's people, he would not be able to distinguish between right and wrong (strengths and weaknesses). So he prayed, "Give me now wisdom and knowledge that I may go out and come in before this people: for who can judge this thy people that is so great?" (2 Chronicles 1:10) Patiently wait on the Lord to be all that he has purposed for you in this world.

Decisiveness of purpose is characterised by firmness on the vision and goal you have decided to pursue in life. However, as believers we need to understand that decisiveness does not mean being stubborn, arrogant or hasty but the ability to decide with speed and clarity in all matters of life.

Ruth made up her mind to follow her mother in-law regardless of the price involved. "And Ruth said, Intreat me not to leave thee, or to return from following after thee: for whither thou goest, I will go; and where thou lodgest, I will lodge: thy people shall be my people, and thy God my God: Where thou diest, will I die, and there will I be buried: the LORD do so to me, and more also, if ought but death part thee and me,"(Ruth 1:16-17)

Ruth was very determined to follow Noami even to the point of death. She had a purpose and a will, despite Naomi trying to dissuade her. She spoke with confidence and resolutely decided to remain with her— she was steadfast about her definite purpose.

Samuel also had the courage to remain faithful to his conviction and purpose (1 Samuel 2:26)

Jeremiah was another example who stood for the purpose he had — to preach the word of the Lord. He decided not to turn back from his visions, goals and the direction he had. (Jeremiah 26:12). He was also not concerned with what the people of that nation would do unto him. He was ready to pay the painful price and go through self-denial to bring his purpose to pass.

We have to be able to deny ourselves at all times when seeking to achieve your purpose in life. Being decisive is simply the most rational way to take on any problem. You observe the information you have available and then you decide what would be the most successful course of action.

If it is possible to get more information, you decide how to get it, because, "Without a decision no progress can be made" as Bishop Hutton-Wood says. If you can't get more data, you simply decide with the facts available.

Although it would be nice if we lived in a world

where perfect information can be retrieved readily, being decisive ultimately means recognising when you already have the best information you are going to get. At this point you simply need to make a decision with the information at hand and move forward. Waiting longer is just delaying the inevitable, so you must decide even in the face of uncertainty.

The word of God cannot lie, what he has promised concerning your destiny, he will do. In every believer's hands lie the seeds of failure or potential for greatness. Your decision regarding your purpose will only be realised depending on your decisiveness of that sure purpose.

I have come to appreciate that "Success is by choice and failure is by choice." All great men and successful people in life make choices and those choices they make either promote their business or collapse it.

In the pursuit of our individual dreams we need to make a choice not to give up along the way but remain focused on the very little dream, business, goal and studies to see it come to pass. Until we become very obsessed with our purpose in life we cannot be successful. (Joshua 1:8)

When all attention, time and total efforts are given to your dreams and purpose you will experience God's extraordinary favour and miracles in your life.

LET US RECAP

❶ Be decisive and remain focused, be like a postage stamp on a letter to your destination.

❷ It is also very important that we fight to remain focused and decisive in anything you set your mind on by building walls that will strengthen your concentration.

❸ Time is a precious thing. Therefore in the process of time, whatever and wherever you sow, it will incredibly grow.

❹ Intimidation and bullying are both methods of getting you to change your mind or your stance on your purpose.

> Your value of knowledge determines your upliftment in life. (DAVID OYEDEPO (JNR)

> The future is secured by those who know how to sharpen, use their gifts and their strength by identifying and making the most of their given opportunities. (BISHOP HUTTON-WOOD)

> Now the Lord blessed the latter days of Job more than his beginning: for he had fourteen thousand sheep, six thousand camels, one thousand yoke of oxen, and one thousand female donkeys. (JOB 42:12)

> Life without a purpose is life without meaning. The greatest tragedy in life is not death, but life without purpose. (DR MYLES MUNROE)

> You don't only have a dream but chase it to its limits and make sure you catch it. (US PRESIDENT BARRACK HUSSEIN OBAMA)

Be like Shadrach, Meshach and Abednego, who made a choice to remain focused and never gave in to intimidation to defile the almighty God.

DON'T CHASE YOUR PENSION; CHASE YOUR DREAM PASSION. 👍

5

No More Limitations

Do not rejoice over me, O my enemy. Though I fall I will rise; though I dwell in darkness, the LORD is a light for me. (MICAH 7:8 NASB)

You bear the sole responsibility for who you are today and who you will become in the future. No one else is responsible for your personal growth and success. According to Clint Eastwood, it is important that, "Men must know their limitations." What are your limitations?

Limitations are any form of rules, situations and circumstances that prevent free movement. It may also be any form of condition(s) that limits an individual's ability to improve, due to a defect, a failing andor short falls. Limitations may come in many forms, some may be imposed by others, some by misconceptions, while others may be self-imposed. Limitations may sometimes exist purely because of our own individual perspectives about life's circumstances.

Nevertheless, as Christians, the way we view our perceived limitations and those of others can affect the manner in which we deal with them. It is very important however that our responses must be through the word of God. It is very true that we may not always be able to control the limitations that could confront us in our daily life, but the possibility is that we can achieve this feat through the powerful word of God.

We may be born with some limitations, while we may acquire some along life's pathway. Jabez, was labelled as "sorrow" at birth because his mother gave birth to him while in pain (1 Chronicles 4:9-11). Here the evidence is that sorrow and pain were the main limitations towards achieving victory or success.

Maybe your life has been associated with painful and sorrowful events, and as you grow older, negative things are being said about you.

Your peers may be calling you names which may be associated with your family history. Some family members may have rejected you because your birth was not what they actually expected.

At times we may suffer certain things or go through certain experiences or challenges of life, not because we originate them but perhaps because of our connections to certain family backgrounds and therefore suffer various degrees of negative labelling and may even be spoken against and called derogatory names. You may also be told in the face you will not succeed in any life pursuits or endeavours. These experiences could limit your progress.

Jabez's life was full of challenging issues. Everywhere he went he was called "sorrow and pain" (1 Chronicles 4: 9-11).

What have you been called? This could be the limiting factor to the progress of your life. The Bible account is that in the process of time Jabez called on the God of Israel, "O that thou wouldest bless me indeed, and enlarge my coast, and that thine hand might be with me, and that thou wouldest keep me from evil, that it may not grieve me."

This is the proverbial Jabez' prayer in 1

Chronicles 4:10. He knew that things were not going on well with him and for him. To make any progress in his life, things had to change!

Jabez did not allow the history of his birth to limit him in any way; he resorted to fellowship and communion with God through the power of prayer. He never focused on the labels and ridicules of his contemporaries, but called upon his God.

I trust that Jabez may have read Psalm 27:10 which says, "When my father and mother forsake me, the Lord will look after me." Obviously, he saw beyond his limitation and the labels, which motivated him to pray this kind of prayer to effect change in his life.

Whatever limitations you may place before the throne of grace, the good Lord will see you through, as his word says, "Call unto me and l will answer you and show you great and mighty things . . ." (Jeremiah 33: 3).

Evidently, no matter the negative opinions and notions that others may hold against you, as you desire change, in the process of time your situation will change in the name of Jesus.

As we grow and mature in life, it is our

responsibility to change the things we dislike or are uncomfortable with.

There is no doubt in my mind that my parents did their best for me as a child, but in the process of time I have come to make certain changes in my personal life. This is because I strongly believe that one has the choice and the responsibility to make necessary changes regarding how one turns up in life, a decision that may change our lives and destinies and impact positively on generations to come.

Therefore until we become restless and obsessed with our present circumstances, we cannot make any changes that may impact positively on the lives of others.

Jabez acknowledged that his family background was different from that of his peers. He understood and appreciated the exigency of paying a price through prayer to effect the needed change in his personal lifestyle. Surely, Jabez may have come to terms with the hard truth that for him to experience a better life, he had to change the things he was saying about himself.

There are four lessons we can learn from Jabez's prayer:

(i) Bless me indeed: Jabez demanded that God should bless him greatly. He knew that the blessing of the Lord maketh rich and added no sorrow (Proverbs 10: 22). He was fully persuaded that only God can change his situation and remove the limitations or labels beyond all that he can ask for or imagine.

(ii) Enlarge my coast: Jabez was requesting that the God of Israel should empower him to maximize his destiny so as to bring joy to him and glory to God. He also acknowledged the fact that some limitations have been placed on his destiny and that to break through, God will have to extend his boundaries and surroundings which can enable him take over and instead of taking cover.

You may have been limited in areas of business or career perhaps due to financial constraints. You may have requested the heavenly father to give you wisdom, understanding, patience, humility, love and joy within your specific spheres of life endeavour or made a request to the effect of divine health so as to stay in perfect health.

Interestingly, so many of us want instant answers to our prayer requests. Yes, it is possible with God, but that is done at his will and time, not ours. It is just a question of time and bingo, you will have testimony to share.

The Bible states clearly in 3 John 1:2, that, "I wish above all things that thou be in good health and prosper. . ." It is God's desire that his children prosper so as to bless others, he told Abraham, "I will make you a great nation, and 1 will bless you, and make your name great; and so you shall be a blessing. (Genesis 12: 2-3)

Another lesson here is that Jabez knew he can reach far more and accomplish more in life so as to make more positive impact. His perception is that God is able to do exceedingly abundantly above all that we ask or think, according to the power that works in us," (Ephesians 3:20)

He desires to fill us with his fullness and to get us out of the way of limitations and failures, as it is not his wish that these shortfalls become our portion.

God's unlimited blessings are also reflected in 2 Kings 4:6, "And it came to pass, when the vessels were full, that she said unto her son, bring me another vessel. And he said unto her, there is not a vessel more, and the oil ceased."

So long as there were vessels to be filled, the miraculous flow of oil continued and it only ceased when there were no more jars to contain it. The lady had just enough vessels to contain the flow of oil, thus she had limited vessels when God has unlimited flow of oil of blessings to change her life and that of her entire generation.

From the account, it was only the number of vessels she had that got filled with the oil — that is the miracle was limited to the available vessels; the prophet who did not speak any word to stop the flow of the oil. Our readiness to allow God to expand our limited ideas, vessels, nets and indeed, our coasts, in making impact can only be made possible if we stop limiting the power of God. No limitation is above God and we should not fail in life, as no amount of limitation under the universe can restrain the blessings of God in our lives.

(iii) THE HAND OF GOD WOULD BE WITH ME: Jabez had no doubt in his mind that the hand of God is so powerful to lead him above his limitations. This knowledge made him to seek God's hand upon his life. He thus was behaving like David as in Psalm 23. He was so desperate that he demanded the hand of God to be with him to lead him, protect, strengthen and demonstrate his works in him; the same hand which took the children of Israel out of Egypt and led them through the red sea to the promised land of milk and honey.

(iv) **KEEP ME FROM EVIL, THAT I MAY NOT CAUSE PAIN:** At times believers pray for miracles and blessings without taking the time to find out the purpose of their requests. There are always reasons for the miracles and blessings that come into our lives. It is very important that we do not allow our miracles and blessings to become a stumbling block between us and our good Lord who makes these provisions abundantly available to us.

Whatever we desire of God, let us remember that it would be within a process of time, within which God may be testing our ability to manage the miracles and the blessings that, that job, child, or promotion etc. will bring.

It is important that we do not allow such the Lord's fulfillment of his promises take away his glory. When this happens we cause pain to our almighty God and as Isaiah 42: 8 tells us, God will not share his glory with any man.

It is in this view that Jabez prayed not to fall into temptation and that evil people should not harm him. It is significant to note here that aspect of Jabez's prayer asking for grace to prevent him causing harm and or pain to others.

The God that answers prayer

Ours is a faithful God who answers prayer. It does not matter how long you may have prayed; what the Lord has promised, he will fulfill in your life. It is just a matter of time. Jabez was very distressed by the wickedness of his day. He therefore acknowledged God as the only power which can deliver him from his personal predicaments and experiences. Hence he cried out to the living Lord and the merciful Lord showed up in his moment of need (1Chronicle 4).

Brethren, be encouraged by the words of Psalm 88.13-15 that the Lord will not hide his face from you. Jeremiah prayed unto the Lord and never focused on his situations or circumstances (Jeremiah 3:24-25).

It does not matter how far you may have gone out of God's plan for your life. If only you can acknowledge his authority and supremacy, recognize your short falls, repent and go back home to him, through repentance and prayer, his divine answers is your portion.

You may be seeking for deliverance from sinful behaviour, sicknesses, divine care and protection from the evils of this wicked world or any other pressing need, just go to the Lord in prayer with one plea and in the process of time (God's time), you will surely receive the answer in Jesus' name- Matthew 7:7-8.

When Peter was arrested and cast into prison, pending execution, as he held on to the faith and brethren continued to pray and await God's divine intervention, in the process of time, God sent an angel who went to the prison to set him free (Acts 12:3-11). Peter's example affirms that when believers seek the face of God and pray, God who has the absolute capacity to remove any limitations on us will manifest his presence in our circumstances.

That limitation may be a statement made concerning your destiny that you will not amount to anything. You may see these words manifesting in your life, use the word of God to cancel it in the name of Jesus our saviour who died on the cross that we may be saved.

The word of God says that, "No weapon that is formed against thee shall prosper, and every tongue that shall rise against thee in judgment thou shalt condemn. This is the heritage of the servants of the Lord, and their righteousness is of me, saith the Lord," (Isaiah 54:17, Romans 8:31)

Several examples abound in the Bible attesting to the truth that God is in the business of answering prayers, having answered – Abraham's desire for a child (Genesis 21:2); Jacob in Genesis 32:33, Gideon in Judges 6:36-40, Samson in Judges 15:18-19, Hezekiah in 2 Kings 20:1-11 and Ezekiel 37.

As you continue to read, it is my prayer that you will be able to identify your limitations and go to God in prayer. He will empower you to rise above whatever limitations there are and God's plans and desires for you will come to pass, "For l know the plans l have for you' declares the Lord, "plans to prosper you and not to harm you, plans to give you hope and a future," (Jeremiah 29:11).

Let us see some Bible characters who rose above their limitations and discouragements:

Elijah was discouraged because of exhaustion. After a great spiritual victory, when he called down fire from heaven and destroyed all the prophets of Baal, one little woman scared him to death because she threatened to kill him. And he was ready to give up. "I have had enough, Lord," he said. "Take my life; I am no better than my ancestors," (1 Kings 19:4).

Hannah was discouraged because the deepest desire of her heart had not been given to her. And it was a good and worthy desire—to have a baby that she could give back to the Lord. Downhearted and discouraged, in bitterness of soul, Hannah wept hard and prayed to the Lord for a baby. (1 Sam. 1)

You may be discouraged because of unfulfilled desires like marriage, but the right person hasn't come along. Maybe, like Hannah, it's the desire to have a baby, but your womb has been closed so far. Maybe it's your dreams of serving God in some special way, but the door hasn't opened yet. It can be discouraging. So, we can certainly see that discouragement is nothing new; it's been around since the beginning of time.

Naomi was discouraged because of financial difficulties and terrible loss. Her husband and two sons had both died, and she was left penniless and homeless. Don't call me Naomi, she told her friends.

Call me Mara (meaning bitter), because the Almighty has made my life very bitter... (Ruth 1:20-21). It's easy enough to understand her discouragement. Financial difficulties cause a great deal of discouragement for many of us.

Mary and Martha were discouraged because they lost someone they loved, and they had really expected Jesus to save him. After all, Jesus had been healing all kinds of other people; surely he would come and save his beloved friend, Lazarus, they reasoned. And when he didn't, they were very discouraged; Jesus had disappointed them. "Lord, Martha said to Jesus, if you had been here, my brother would not have died (John 11:21).

Have you ever set an agenda out for the Lord, expecting him to work on your time table, and then been disappointed when he didn't come through? It can be very discouraging.

Peter was discouraged because of his own failure. After he denied the Lord three times, Peter went out and wept bitterly. I imagine he felt that he had blown it for good, and he must have been terribly discouraged with himself. How could he deny the Lord, the one he promised never to deny?

When I look at myself and see how inadequate I am, how often I fail, how I go back and do the same things over and over that I know I shouldn't do, I get very discouraged. In fact, that discourages me probably more than anything else, how about you?

Jesus fought discouragement when his friends failed him; when he was misunderstood; when he tried to help and his help was refused. That really hurts, when you have totally good motives, and yet people don't approve or understand or support you. In fact, they may reject you, as they did Jesus.

Well, it is encouraging to see that even these great people of God went through times of discouragement. If you've been discouraged lately, you've probably also felt guilty about being discouraged. But it's good to remember that everyone goes through periods of discouragement. I think it's important to emphasize that being discouraged is not a sin.

God uses people who are discouraged; God understands discouragement; discouragement is a normal and unavoidable emotion that we must all deal with. It comes to us in different ways, for different reasons, and at different times, but rest assured that the grace of God is sufficient for us in times of discouragement and he will surely see us through if we faint not.

Paul tells us, "And he said unto me, my grace is sufficient for thee: for my strength is made perfect in weakness. Most gladly therefore will I rather glory in my infirmities, that the power of Christ may rest upon me," 2 Corinthians 12:9.

LET US RECAP:

1. In the process of time, as things were not going too well with Jabez, he made a conscious effort to have a change of his life story, which he believed could only be done by God and with God.

2. Although Jabez was limited, he knew that God is unlimited, reminding us that we cannot think the same as God, as his ways are not ours and are above our ways. His thoughts are above our thoughts, his love we can grow in, but never grasp fully.

3. God is in the business of answering the prayers of his people in all circumstances at all times,

provided we are humble enough to turn away from our sins and go to him in prayer and faith, believing that whatsoever we ask of the Lord, it will be granted, (John 14: 13-14).

4. Remember that you are the prophet of your own destiny and it is when you have discovered yourself and begin to take steps of faith, develop the right mindset and positive attitude to effect change in your personal life that life becomes meaningful.

5. God wants you to prosper and be in excellent health, just call unto him and he will show you the way, but you must be born again. Go for it, denounce your past, and accept Jesus now as your personal saviour and all your limitations will melt away.

Some Quotations to Encourage You:

> If my people which are called by my name shall humble themselves and pray and seek my face and turn from their wicked ways, then l will hear from heaven, and will forgive their sin, and will heal their land. (2 CHRONICLES 7:14)

> For lack of knowledge my people are destroyed. (HOSEA 4: 6)

> The future is what you make it and not what you think it should be, but is created by those who turn adversity into advantage and do not allow their past to hold their life hostage" (BISHOP MICHAEL HUTTON-WOOD)

> When purpose is unknown, abuse is inevitable. (BISHOP HUTTON-WOOD)

We worship a God who is above all limitations and he is an ever faithful and prayer answering father.

REMEMBER, ALL THINGS ARE POSSIBLE WITH OUR GOD. 👍

6

Don't Give Up: You Have A Sure Future

But the path of the just is as the shining light, that shineth more and more unto the perfect day.
(PROVERB 1:18)

In the early stages of pregnancy, a baby is likely to be lost. This also applies to our God-given dream; therefore we need to protect it and ensure it is preserved. The enemy tried so hard to destroy Moses and Jesus before they reached their second birthdays. Why? Because the enemy feared their future, just as he fears yours.

When a prospective mother is pregnant, she has to do certain things in order to have a safe delivery. But some pregnant women drink alcohol, smoke and eat certain types of food detrimental to the baby's health. Why can you not do the same? The answer is that what you are carrying is different from what they are carrying. Your dream is different from theirs.

Remember that, pursuing your dream requires you daring to be different. You may even shave to make some radical changes but you have to do it to see your dream come true. Sometimes it will demand that you disconnect from some relationship and habits that can hurt you. It will also require you to stay out of certain places and reorder your priorities according to your God-given destiny, not popular consent.

Esther's vision meant that she decided to put her life on the line, saying, "If perish, I perish." She did not even perish even though she was willing to die for her vision.

It is sometimes shocking to know that some people wear themselves out trying to fulfill a vision God did not give them just to win or demonstrate that they are as talented as their peers, siblings or their parents.

When we look at Abraham's life, he had to

learn a hard lesson when God promised him a son. He was so impatient with God and worried about getting old. He took a bad decision following his wife's bad advice and ended up fathering Ishmael. Abraham had to live with the outcome of his decision for the rest of his life.

People who make this mistake end up with a sense of failure and frustration because they are constantly measuring themselves by somebody else's assignment. It is very important that each and every one of us identify our individual talent and gifts that can help us fulfill our dreams. Remember that a man's individual gifts are what brings him before great men and opens door for him. (Proverbs 18:16). The president of a bank will entertain large depositors, and a senator will golf with you for a sizable campaign contribution.

It is clear that without a clear purpose in life, one can only be changing directions, jobs, relationships, churches, etc. hoping that each change they make will make them settle down. This is a pure lack of focus.

Scientists have discovered that with a magnifying glass, the rays of the sun can set paper on fire. But when the light is focused on even more as a laser beam, it can cut through steel.

In Philippians 3:13-14, Paul made it clear that, "Brethren, I do not count myself to have apprehended; but one thing I do, forgetting those things which are behind and reaching forward to those things which are ahead, I press toward the goal for the prize of the upward call of God in Christ Jesus."

We discover here that Paul was very focused on his dream of making Christ known to the world. Therefore if we want our lives to be impactful then we all need to remain focused on our dreams.

Sometimes our fellow brethren can point out something that we may be doing wrong. Don't get upset. Be honest and ask yourself, could they be right; then pray to God and see to make changes that will make you a better person.

Watch, stand fast in the faith, be brave, and be strong. This is what 1 Corinthians 16:13 says. As Christians striving to live the way God wants us to live, we always have to be watchful as to the many ways of sin that are all around us. We have to stand fast and resist the desire to fall into the traps that the enemy is trying to set for us.

Every day we should acknowledge that we need God. When we start to act like we do not need God in our lives and that we can do everything ourselves, that's when we run into problems. Acknowledging God makes our situation bearable. We have to realize what our purpose is in God; only then can our lives take on new meaning and work towards the destiny God has for us.

In the pursuit of destiny, many things may catch your eye but keep your single eye on the very purpose for your life.

People may be describing you by your past, family members may be remembering your bad behaviour during your childhood but I can guarantee you that you are more than what they think they know. Your days of tears will be over soon because, "Weeping may endure for a night, but joy cometh in the morning."(Psalm 30:5)

I want to assure you that for any form of reproach, regret, disappointment, or failure which causes you to weep, the Lord God is contending on your behalf, so hold your peace in Jesus' name.

The Lord is saying that you are his battle axe and weapon of war with which he will destroy kingdoms, (Jeremiah 51:20) so just remain focused.

No matter where you have been, no matter where you are at this moment, if you have not yet found God's plans for your life, please stop what you are doing and start looking for it; begin where you are right now. God is ready to put your life back on track. He is ready to give you a sense of hope. "For I know the thoughts that I think toward you, saith the LORD, thoughts of peace, and not of evil, to give you an expected end." (Jeremiah 29:11)

You may be wondering, "Am I ever going to fulfill my destiny? Why have I not married yet? Why are others getting good jobs and building houses and you have not even asked for the price of bricks? Well the good news is that God is preparing you for something great. The word of God says that, "For the vision is yet for an appointed time, but at the end it shall speak, and not lie: though it tarry, wait for it; because it will surely come, it will not tarry." (Habakkuk 2:2-3).

We need to understand that, everything has its moment and cycle — some in an hour and some in a century; but the very purpose of that particular thing (dreams, plans, education, childbirth) shall surely complete their cycle, whether long or short.

Brethren, instead of focusing on our problems, it is very important that we look to our God and trust his word. Psalm 34:19 encourages us that, "Many are the afflictions of the righteous: but the Lord delivereth him out of them all."

Furthermore, God's assurance to us is that, "When thou passest through the waters, I will be with thee; and through the rivers, they shall not overflow thee: when thou walkest through the fire, thou shalt not be burned; neither shall the flame kindle upon thee." (Isaiah 43:2).

LET US RECAP:

1. Focusing on your past histories or background will only hinder you from seeing the future. No matter how long and depressing the past was, just look ahead.
2. It is only a God-given hope that can sustain us through difficult and trying times.
3. While God wants us to move forward in his love and learn more about him and his son Jesus Christ, the devil doesn't like it, so he sends negative situations against you.

❹ Do not despise or lose your precious dreams only to seek it diligently with tears. If you stay focused and right on track, you will get to where you want to be.

❺ We need to be very disciplined to remain focus and not get distracted by any wind of doctrine or the affairs of this world.

Some Quotations to Encourage You:

> There is hope for you and will bud, and bring forth boughs like a plant. (JOB 14:9)

> And it shall come to pass that whosoever shall call on the name of the Lord shall be saved. (ACTS 2:21)

> New levels bring new devils. (UNKNOWN)

> But we all, with open face beholding as in a glass the glory of the Lord, are changed in the same image from glory to glory even as by the spirit of the Lord. (CORINTHIANS 3:18)

God's purposes and plans for your life will not be cut off but it will surely come to pass in your life.

REMEMBER, NOTHING IS POTENT AS A FOCUSED LIFE. 👍

7

Be Still: God Is Fighting For You

Ye shall not need to fight in this battle: set yourselves, stand ye still, and see the salvation of the Lord with you, O fear not, nor be dismayed; tomorrow go out against them: for the Lord will be with you. (2 Chronicles 20:17)

Beloved, God is fighting your battles for you. No matter what you may be going through right now, know that you are not in it alone. You may feel tired of "going through". You may be wondering just what next to do and how next to pray. Be encouraged today. God will fight your battle for you.

The enemy is waging war against the body of Christ but he is already defeated. He may be doing all he can to convince you that God is not coming through for you. Maybe he is making it appear as if God is not hearing your prayers, much less answering them, but know that the devil is a liar.

God is for you. He is with you and he knows exactly what you are experiencing at this time. He has not left you and he will not leave you now.

Now more than ever, be determined that come what may, you will serve the Lord. You see, your destiny in Jesus Christ is sure, as long as you continue to trust God and you do not faint.

God has great things in store for your life. He has already told you about many of the things that He has in store for you. He has shown them to you in dreams and visions.

He has spoken them to you through prophetic words and by his still small voice. God is able to bring to pass the vision that he has placed within you, to further his kingdom.

Beloved, do not become discouraged by the war that is raging around you. Call on the Lord who is mighty to deliver you. Do not bow to pressures or attacks. The power of God is great, and greater is the Lord Jesus Christ who is in you.

Yes, it may seem like it is long in coming but know that God will manifest mighty blessings in your life. Keep focused and be fervent in prayer as you serve the Lord. Do not grow weary in well doing. Increase your time of praise and worship, fasting and prayer. Give thanks to God.

Beloved, God is more than able to do all that he has promised you. Maybe, things did not quite work out the way that you thought they would in some areas but God is not dead. He is very much alive. His ways are higher than your ways.

You must believe that even what seems to be bad is working together for good because you love God and you are called by the Lord.

In the midst of your struggles, encourage others in the Lord. Do not become consumed with what is coming against you. For there are many hurting, many lonely, many lost and many discouraged who are waiting for you to share a word of hope with them. As you minister to them even in your pain, God will minister to you... give and it shall be given to you...

Remember the battle on Mount Carmel and know that the God who answered by fire is your

God. In the midst of your fire he is sure to answer with his fire which gives power, and destroys the works of the enemy. 2 Corinthians 10:4 says, "The weapons of our warfare are not carnal, they are mighty in God. . ."

We as the children of God have the *four* mighty weapons:

(i) the word of the living God
(ii) the name of Jesus (the name above every name)
(iii) the power of prayer and
(iv) the power of praise and worship.

Every believer can become a winner. We are not fighting a losing battle. There is no temptation that comes against us that we cannot overcome. We need not be intimidated by what others would think but on the contrary, be concerned about what God will think.

When Joshua led the people to march around the city of Jericho, they had to be silent. They had to refuse to speak negative things of doubt and fear. They were in an attitude of "waiting on God". (Joshua 6: 1-5)

This is what we need to learn to do when we

wage a war against the enemy. We should quit talking words of fear and anxiety. The Lord taught them patience too. They had to do it seven days. This is so important because we cannot hurry God into anything. Finally, they shouted with a great shout. That, is praise!

Some battles are won by prayer, patience and praise. The Lord has promised us the victory. What is the battle you are going through? It may be your family or finances or your health. Trust in the Lord! He will honour your faith. He will come through. Never give up. The battle belongs to the Lord and the victory belongs to you. You are more than a conqueror in Christ Jesus. Greater is he that is in you than he that is in this world! Amen.

Beloved be confident today that the weapons that have been formed against you will not prosper. God is faithful.

The conclusion of the matter. . .

No matter what our background was, when we start to trust and depend on God daily, and work through our past hurts resolutely, then we have hope for the future. God is not too late to change your situation around.

You need to do the ridiculous to receive the miraculous. God is all you need to have all you needs met. The secret of your future lies in your daily routine. Therefore what you think about yourself today regarding your background will always determine how you view and embrace the future.

Regretting something is another form of not accepting reality. What can you do about it now? It's gone. It does not exist anymore. Let us all begin to focus on what we can change and do better.

Once we have resolved our past hurts, it is not what we have or don't have that matters in life, but what we do with what we have. God wants us to acknowledge past hurts so that we do not repeat the same mistakes but to grow through them. In so doing, our future will not be controlled by our past.

When people move on, you too move on and ensure that they do not come back to meet you at the very same spot they left you. Don't regret your past. Live for today, but with tomorrow in mind.

The past is gone but the future is what you do with the past to catapult you into your sure destiny.

*It is therefore up to us what
we do about the present.*

YOU ARE A CHILD OF DESTINY. IT IS THE
WILL OF GOD THAT YOU BE IN
HEALTH AND PROSPER.

VICTORY IS YOURS.

Inspirational Hymns

Let Your Living Water Flow Over My Soul

Let Your living water flow over my soul
Let Your Holy Spirit come and take control
Of every situation that has troubled my mind
All my cares and burdens on to You I roll

Jesus, Jesus, Jesus
Father, Father, Father
Spirit, Spirit, Spirit

Come now, Holy Spirit, and take control
Hold me in Your loving arms and make me whole
Wipe away all doubt and fear and take my pride
Draw me to Your love and keep me by Your side

Give your life to Jesus, let Him fill your soul
Let Him take you in His arms and make you whole
As you give your life to Him He'll set you free
You will live and reign with Him eternally

© 1986 Ampelos Music

Higher Ground

I'm pressing on the upward way,
New heights I'm gaining every day;
Still praying as I'm onward bound,
"Lord, plant my feet on higher ground."

Lord, lift me up and let me stand,
By faith, on heaven's table land,
A higher plane than I have found;
Lord, plant my feet on higher ground.

My heart has no desire to stay
Where doubts arise and fears dismay;
Though some may dwell where those abound,
My prayer, my aim, is higher ground.

Refrain

I want to live above the world,
Though Satan's darts at me are hurled;
For faith has caught the joyful sound,
The song of saints on higher ground.

Refrain

I want to scale the utmost height
And catch a gleam of glory bright;
But still I'll pray till Heav'n I've found,
"Lord, plant my feet on higher ground."

Refrain

© 1898 Words by Johnson Oatman, Jr.
© 1898 Music by Charles H. Gabriel

Renew Your Mind

Isaiah 43:18-19 (NIV)
Forget the former things; do not dwell on the past. See, I am doing a new thing! Now it springs up; do you not perceive it? I am making a way in the desert and streams in the wasteland.

Philippians 3:12-14 (NKJV)
Not that I have already attained, or am already perfected; but I press on, that I may lay hold of that for which Christ Jesus has also laid hold of me. Brethren, I do not count myself to have apprehended; but one thing I do, forgetting those things which are behind and reaching forward to those things which are ahead, I press toward the goal for the prize of the upward call of God in Christ Jesus.

Jeremiah 29:11 (KJV)
For I know the thoughts that I think toward you, saith the LORD, thoughts of peace, and not of evil, to give you an expected end.

2 Corinthians 5:17 (KJV)
Therefore if any man be in Christ, he is a new creature: old things are passed away; behold, all things are become new.

Job 17:9 (NLT)
The righteous keep moving forward, and those with clean hands become stronger and stronger.

Romans 8:1(KJV)
There is therefore now no condemnation to them which are in Christ Jesus, who walk not after the flesh, but after the Spirit.

Hebrews 12:1(KJV)
Therefore, since we are surrounded by so great a cloud of witnesses, let us also lay aside every weight, and sin which clings so closely, and let us run with endurance the race that is set before us, looking to Jesus, the founder and perfecter of our faith, who for the joy that was set before him endured the cross, despising the shame, and is seated at the right hand of the throne of God.

Galatians 2:20 (KJV)
I am crucified with Christ: nevertheless I live; yet not I, but Christ liveth in me: and the life which I now live in the flesh I live by the faith of the Son of God, who loved me, and gave himself for me.

1 Peter 2:1-2 (NRSV)
Rid yourselves, therefore, of all malice, and all guile, insincerity, envy, and all slander. Like newborn infants, long for the pure, spiritual milk,

so that by it you may grow into salvation — if indeed you have tasted that the Lord is good. Come to him, a living stone, though rejected by mortals yet chosen and precious in God's sight, and like living stones, let yourselves be built* into a spiritual house, to be a holy priesthood, to offer spiritual sacrifices acceptable to God through Jesus Christ.

1 Peter 2:2 (KJV)
As newborn babes, desire the sincere milk of the word, that ye may grow thereby.

Philippians 3:12 (NASB)
Not that I have already obtained it or have already become perfect, but I press on so that I may lay hold of that for which also I was laid hold of by Christ Jesus.

Psalm 119:105 (KJV)
Thy word is a lamp unto my feet, and a light unto my path.

Psalm 119:11 (KJV)
Thy words have I hid in mine heart that I might not sin against thee.

Isaiah 40:31 (NIV)
But those who hope in the LORD, will renew their strength. They will soar on wings like eagles; they

will run and not grow weary, they will walk and not be faint.

Psalm 31:24 (KJV)
Be of good courage, and he shall strengthen your heart, all ye that hope in the LORD.

Proverbs 16:3 (NASB)
Commit your works to the LORD and your plans will be established.

Luke 9:23 (KJV)
And he said to them all, If any man will come after me, let him deny himself, and take up his cross daily, and follow me.

Philippians 4:1 (KJV)
Therefore, my brethren dearly beloved and longed for, my joy and crown, so stand fast in the Lord, my dearly beloved.

Philippians 1:6 (KJV)
Being confident of this very thing, that he which hath begun a good work in you will perform it until the day of Jesus Christ.

Romans 12:2 (NLT)
Don't copy the behavior and customs of this world, but let God transform you into a new person by

changing the way you think. Then you will learn to know God's will for you, which is good and pleasing and perfect.

Jeremiah 29:11(KJV)
For I know the thoughts that I think toward you, saith the LORD, thoughts of peace, and not of evil, to give you an expected end.

References

Abioye, David O., (Books) *Productive Thinking; Overcoming Stagnation*

Hutton-Wood, Michael Bishop Dr., *(Books) Leadership Capsules; I Shall Rise Again; How to Negotiate Your Desired Future With Today's Currency; You Need to Do the Ridiculous to Experience the Miraculous; 175 Reasons Why You Cannot Fail.*

Jones, Rhonda, *You Must Change Your Mind to Change Your Life.*

Oyedepo, David Dr., *Understanding Vision, In Pursuit of Vision.*

Rayan, Jemima, *Become a Winner.*

Roua, Dragos, *100 Ways to in Prove Your Life.*

Walter Staples Dr., *How to Think Like a Winner.*

Whelchel, Mary, *Defeating Discouragement.*

www.ingramcontent.com/pod-product-compliance
Lightning Source LLC
Chambersburg PA
CBHW071308040426
42444CB00009B/1922